Top Gear

EPIC FAILURES

RICHARD PORTER

BBC
BOOKS

Contents

TopGear

Designing and making cars is an expensive thing to do. So is racing them. All told, the car business spends billions every year and with such vast sums at stake you'd think the people involved wouldn't give desk space to Captain Cockup. Sadly, you would be wrong.

Every department in every car firm and motorsport operation is capable of complete and abject failure, and on a surprisingly regular basis.

Which is what this book is about. You see, *Top Gear* knows a thing or two about embarrassing mistakes, as anyone who watched our India special will know. The truth is, for many years *Top Gear* has also regarded failure as funny. Where other television programmes edit out the moment where the presenter falls over or slams their hand in a door, *Top Gear* gleefully leaves it in.

So who better to take you on a gentle canter through 50 of the car world's biggest and most glorious failures? That's right, it's *Top Gear*. Who else did you think? If you want this sort of stuff from *Countryfile* you might be in for a wait.

FORD HAS A PONY IDEA

I n the mid-1950s Ford decided to invent a whole new car company which it called Edsel. Not in itself a bad idea, but one made completely rubbish by the actual car it sold, which was badly made and had a front grille that looked uncomfortably like a lady's nether parts. As a result Edsel showrooms were quieter than a Dutch mountaineering shop.

Then the marketing department had a brilliant idea; they would put something in every showroom that would attract children. When children demanded a closer look, the logic said, their parents would follow and give the salesmen at least a fighting chance of selling them a car that resembled a fanny. So what was the child-catcher device Edsel settled on? Balloons? An amusing clown? Some sort of water slide? No, it was a real, live pony.

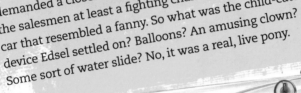

PARENTAL ADVISORY EXPLICIT IMAGERY

Unsurprisingly, this was a terrible idea, not least because car salesmen are not especially well equipped to look after a small horse, nor indeed were they very pleased to find their showrooms suddenly full of straw and poo. Worst of all, when the pony campaign had finished, no one at Ford head office had even considered how they were going to get rid of several hundred redundant ponies. Presumably for the next few months they never ran out of glue.

VAG-1NA

TopGear
EPIC FAILURES

Pedro de la River

The 2002 Formula 1 season was going pretty badly for Jaguar driver Pedro De La Rosa. His car was slow, difficult to drive and it kept breaking down. This run of rotten luck reached a new low during the American Grand Prix at Indianapolis when once again the sluggish Jag decided it couldn't be bothered running race distance and decided to eat its own gearbox. Then it caught fire, just for good measure.

Pulling off to the side of the track, De La Rosa jumped from the car and cursed the gods of motor racing until a friendly race marshal arrived on the scene and told the furious driver to get to a place of safety by leaping over the small wall behind him. De La Rosa obediently did as he was told, which was unfortunate because the marshal had forgotten to mention that on the other side of that wall was a small river.

De La Rosa later described the incident as 'unbelievable', although not as unbelievable as for the Jaguar team who were shocked to see the first recorded incident of a driver escaping a burning car and somehow arriving back in the pits dripping with water.

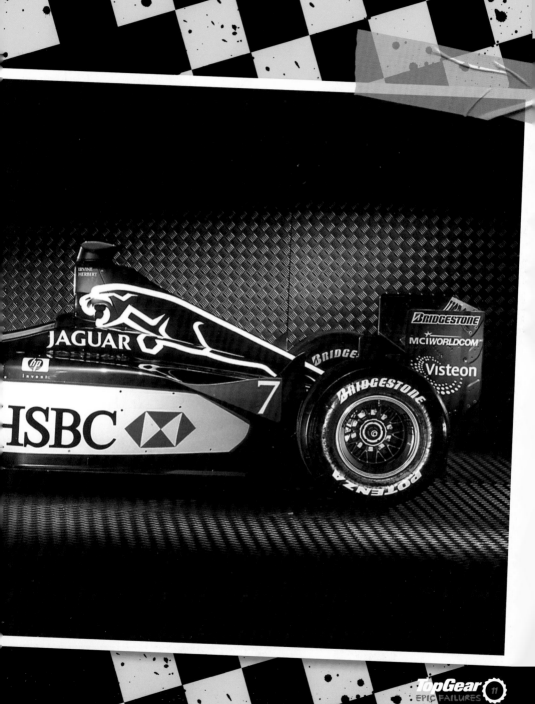

DOWN UNDERWHELMING

I n the 1970s, Leyland wasn't just a British company famed for its strike-wracked factories and occasional eccentric car line up. Leyland had international interests too, not least a whole Australian branch office which had become tired of building and selling designs from the old country. The Aussies wanted permission to create two brand-new models, exclusively for themselves. Steady on, said UK head office in the face of such brazen colonial ambition. You can have some money to do a big car, said the bosses, and for a medium sized one, here are the plans for the Morris Marina. A mixed success for the Aussies then. But they plugged ahead with the flagship saloon which went on sale in June 1973, badged as the P76.

It was certainly large, boasting seats for six and a boot big enough to take a 44 gallon steel drum. Apparently Australians wanted this

IT CAME FREE WITH THESE *STRIDES*.

I'M LEAVING YOU.

as much as they wanted suspension built to survive rough outback roads and a top-of-the-range 4.4-litre V8. The P76 also came with some jaunty, tongue-in-cheek names for the various paint colours including 'Hairy Lime' green, 'Peel Me A Grape' purple and a shade of brown called 'Oh Fudge'.

Those were the good bits. On the downside, Aussies already had their big Holdens and Fords and were suspicious of a new rival from a British company with a reputation for lousy reliability. It didn't help that, from a distance, the P76 badge on the bootlid appeared to say PIG.

The biggest problem for the P76, however, was that by the time it went on sale British Leyland was completely broke. The car had to be an instant runaway hit and when it wasn't desperate British bosses pulled the rug from under their entire Aussie outpost. P76 production ended in October 1974, just 16 months after it had started.

An even crueler fate met the planned coupe version, called the Force 7, which was about to hit showrooms when the factory was shuttered. A few dozen had been built when the bad news came through, all but 10 of which were then taken around the back of the doomed factory and crushed.

Three LITRES OF FAILURE

At the dawn of the 1960s Austin decided it needed a flagship saloon car. They then spent a great deal of time farting about until finally, in 1968, their top-of-the-range saloon went on sale. It was called the 3-litre and it was greeted with an extraordinary wave of apathy.

The problems were various. First of all, captains of industry and other customers wanted to ride around in the lap of luxury whereas the 3-litre's interior was as lavish as a monk's lavatory. Secondly, although it had a three litre engine, as its name implied, it was put on sale with a measly 118 horsepower which made performance leisurely at best. A prototype was built with a Rover V8 engine which would have solved this at a stroke, but Rover themselves were part of the same company, also made large cars for important people, and had a territorial hissy fit until the plan was aborted.

OOH 556G

Finally, and most seriously, the 3-litre looked like a crudely elongated version of the much cheaper Austin 1800. It even used the same doors leading people to believe it was no more than a badly tarted up version of a family saloon. In fact, it was almost completely different underneath. What Austin had achieved, therefore, was the exact opposite of car industry holy grail: They'd spent a load of money coming up with something that looked like they'd spent no money at all.

Things got even worse for the 3-litre when legendary Mini designer and Austin's in-house genius, Alec Issigonis, made it quite clear that this car was nothing to do with him. With such a ringing lack of endorsement on top of its other issues, the 3-litre remained firmly stuck to the showroom floor, suffering feeble sales until, after just three years, Austin pulled the plug.

DOWNWARD SLIDE

The door has been around for centuries and generally the idea is always the same. Put some hinges at one end, a latch at the other, Bob's your dad's brother. It's simple and effective, especially on a car where it stops water getting in and things falling out. Really, there's no logical reason to mess with this formula. But Peugeot thought otherwise and in 2004 announced a new small car with sliding doors.

Not just any sliding doors either. These were electrically powered and could be opened from afar using a button on the key. As it turned out, this was a good thing because if you waited until you arrived at the car itself the achingly slow motors would see you standing in the pouring rain for what felt like half an hour, miserably watching people with normal cars opening their normal doors and getting in as normal.

And there were many other problems with the 1007's door setup. The extra weight of the sliding system made the whole car heavy and that in turn made performance almost imperceptible to the naked eye. The motors developed a reputation for frequent and inconvenient malfunction. And although the electrically powered part of the doors was disabled at speed, you could still open the doors manually whilst driving at 70mph and then find they were impossible to close again. Peugeot claimed this last feature was deliberate in case you needed to open the doors in an emergency whilst driving along although it's impossible to think what that might be, short of one of the car's occupants releasing a truly explosive fart.

Car buyers were not fooled by the 1007. In Britain it lasted just three years before being deleted. It soldiered on a little longer on mainland Europe, but still tanked to such an extent that in five whole years it sold less than Peugeot thought it could shift in 12 months.

The 1007 was nothing short of a slowly sliding failure.

NORFOLK UP

The original 1960s Lotus Elan was a tiny, lightweight two seater that did much to define the Norfolkian sports car-ists reputation for years to come. So when, in the 1980s, Lotus decided to build a brand-new two seater with the Elan name, there was much to live up to. This might explain why they made not one but two false starts, one of which made it to the running prototype stage before being binned.

Attempt three was more successful, despite various problems during its development. This included back lights that were too dim to pass government roadworthiness tests and had to be replaced at short notice by some off-the-shelf Renault items spotted on screen by the chief designer whilst watching '80s yacht toss *Howard's Way* at home one Sunday evening.

There was, however, a rather larger failure when the first production cars were put together in late '89 and came out looking a bit odd. It turned out the people who did all the measurements for the fibreglass body moulds had followed normal procedure and carefully compensated for the amount by which this material would shrink as it dried. But no one had told them that the new Elan would be moulded in the very latest, state-of-the-art fibreglass. Which doesn't shrink. As a result, the Elan's shell was simply too big, making its wheels look lost underneath the oversized body, and there was nothing Lotus could do to fix it.

Looking like a child wearing an adult's hat clearly didn't help the Elan and nor did being front-wheel-drive in a world that expects its sports cars to drive their back wheels. Factor in the faltering economy of the early '90s and the Elan was doomed to fail. Less than three years after it was announced, Lotus abruptly pulled the plug.

Then, two years later, it lurched back into production, billed as a limited run of 800 which actually translated as 'we found 800 engines in a warehouse and we need to get shot of the bloody things'.

Once the engines were gone, the Elan was no more... until Lotus flogged the design to Kia who fitted their own engine, did ruinous things to the suspension and put it on sale in South Korea for three disastrous years. In 1999 the Elan finally died for good.

Despite many failures in its life, it was a decent car. But this was still for the best.

FIAT FAIL

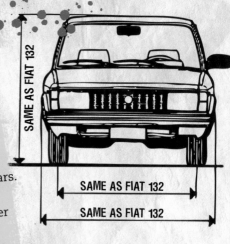

SAME AS FIAT 132

SAME AS FIAT 132

SAME AS FIAT 132

Fiat is tremendously good at making small cars. The original 500. The new 500. The Panda, the 127, the list goes on. Large cars, on the other hand, are something that eludes them. Recent history is littered with examples of bigger Fiats that, thanks to poor design, inept engineering or rampant customer apathy, made little more than a blip on international sales charts. Yet even by the woeful standards of their heftier models, the Argenta marks a particular low point, especially in the UK.

For one thing, it was not the new car it claimed to be, being little more than a crude spruce-up of the saloon, first seen in 1972 and approaching a decade old by the time it was cheaply reheated to make this. The new badge, Argenta, was meant to remind Italian speakers of the precious metal silver but might as well have meant 'leftovers'.

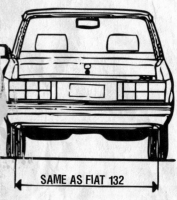

SAME AS FIAT 132

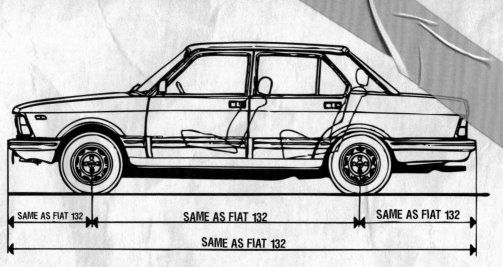

SAME AS FIAT 132   SAME AS FIAT 132   SAME AS FIAT 132

SAME AS FIAT 132

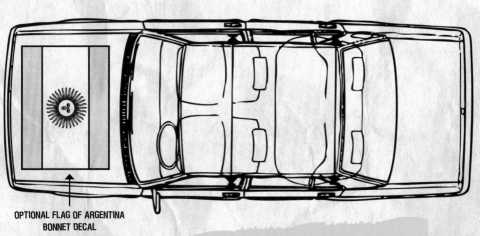

OPTIONAL FLAG OF ARGENTINA
BONNET DECAL

The Argenta was shown off in its homeland in the summer of 1981 but by the time it made it to the UK it had epic failure written all over it. Not only because it was a large Fiat, but also because in April 1982 the Falklands conflict officially began and Britain was at war with Argentina. As UK supermarkets quietly hid their corned beef, here was Fiat proudly hawking a new car with a name that sounded worryingly similar to that of Britain's latest foe.

Sales of big Fiats have never been huge in Britain but with its unfortunately timed name the Argenta was the biggest failure of them all and by 1985 it was no more. Unlike corned beef, which happily bounced back.

HOT MESS

In the late 1960s Ford of America became panicked that European and Japanese rivals were cleaning up in the small car market and came up with a scheme to bring in a smaller, lighter addition to its range. This new car had to be cheap and it had to be rushed into production before those goddam bastards from Volkswagen, Honda and Toyota had the whole market sown up.

It's these last two points that eventually made the Pinto one of the most notorious American cars in history. First of all, instead of taking the car from designer's doodle to actual lump of metal in the usual three or four years, the Pinto was on showroom floors in under two. This meant signing off designs was done in a rush and when a potentially lethal fault was found Ford ignored a simple fix because it added a few dollars to the build cost of each car and knackered their wafer-thin profit projections.

Instead, the Pinto went on sale in late 1970

fitted with a fuel tank that, in a rear end collision, would sheer away from its own filler pipe and become skewered by bolts on the rear axle, haemorrhaging flammable liquid onto the ground. Strangely, the glitzy ads for the new car didn't mention this.

In fact, no one mentioned this until 1977 when US news magazine *Mother Jones* ran a story exposing the Pinto's fatal flaws. Worse yet, the article claimed that Ford had run a cost-benefit analysis around crash safety and decided that it was cheaper simply to deal with the lawsuits and compensation resulting from deaths and injuries than to fix the actual car.

After '77 the Pinto was made more resistant to rear end shunts, but the damage was done, especially to Ford's reputation. The car stayed in production until 1980 but with one other change. Ford's ad agency tactfully dropped a radio ad that said, 'Pinto leaves you with that warm feeling'.

BAH-hA-

It's normal practice in the car industry to design and test a new model in complete secret, tease a few tantalising details, go for a big reveal and then make sure the car is in your showrooms shortly afterwards. What's not normally done is to hire a stand at the Paris Motor Show and simultaneously announce not one but five brand-new cars, even though not one of these new models is even close to going on sale.

Yet, in 2010, that is exactly what Lotus did as it entered a bizarre era under the stewardship of a man called Dany Bahar. And this motor show madness was just the start. During a two year reign of strangeness, Bahar hired an 'ex-Ferrari' chief designer whose most prominent work to date was actually a Citroen people carrier, started publishing a Lotus lifestyle magazine full of beautiful pictures but precious little information, opened an insanely irrelevant Lotus clothes shop on London's Regent Street and gave the job of Vice President of Creative Design & Global Marketing to an American rapper.

All of which would have been excusable if one or two of the five cars he'd announced at the Paris show had subsequently gone on sale. But they hadn't. And the existing range of cars was dead in the water because he'd now told everyone that new stuff was coming soon. Which, in truth, it wasn't. It takes time to develop new car models. Especially five of them. That's why people tend not to announce them years before they're going to be ready.

ha-haAAA

All this nonsense then came to an abrupt end when Lotus accused Dany Bahar of making unauthorised expenses claims and had to let him go. Bahar hit back, crying unfair dismissal and at the time of writing, the situation hasn't been resolved.

One thing is settled, however: The five Lotus models announced with great fanfare at the 2010 Paris Motor Show have now been cancelled. And probably shouldn't have been announced in the first place.

'A NICE LIGHT CAR'

Kimi Raikkonen is brilliant. He refuses to answer idiotic questions, he sometimes looks a bit 'refreshed' and falls off the top of a yacht (look it up on YouTube), and he covertly enters snowmobile races using the pseudonym 'James Hunt'. Also, he's quite good at driving.

But one of his finest moments came at the 2006 Brazilian Grand Prix following a pre-race tribute to retiring world champion Michael Schumacher, led by a local sporting legend. Live on air, ex-racer turned commentator Martin Brundle approached the mumbling Finnish driver to see why he wasn't around for this emotional landmark moment. This is what happened next:

Brundle: Kimi, you missed the presentation by Pele.
Raikkonen: Yeah.
Brundle: Will you get over it?
Raikkonen: [laughs] Yeah, I will. [brightly] I was having a shit.
Brundle: Okay, thanks for that.

Brundle made a quick witted recovery by noting that Raikkonen would have 'a nice light car' for the race but the real punch line belonged to Kimi.

This isn't in any way an epic failure on the Finnish driver's part. It's here because of the ashen-faced, lump-throated reaction it must have provoked in ITV F1 producers who would get slapped wrists for transmitting a mild swear on daytime telly. For Kimi it was another moment of enormous success.

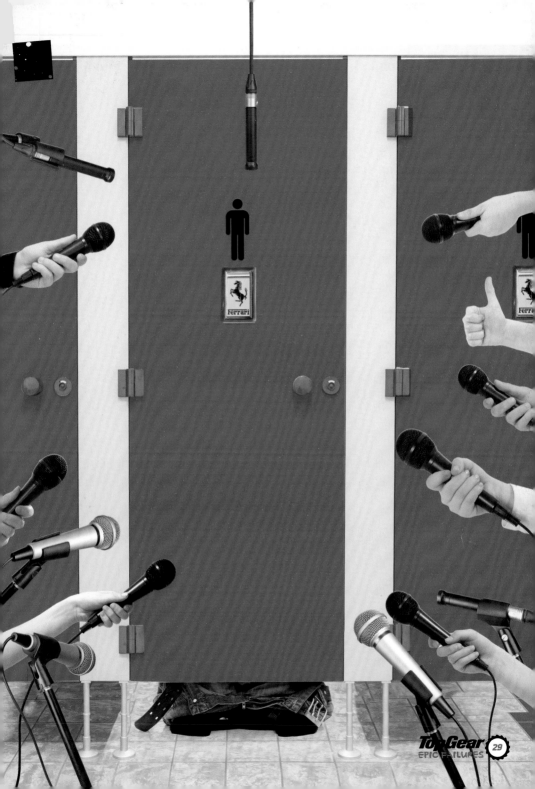

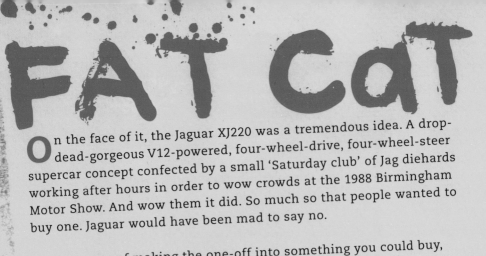

FAT Cat

On the face of it, the Jaguar XJ220 was a tremendous idea. A drop-dead-gorgeous V12-powered, four-wheel-drive, four-wheel-steer supercar concept confected by a small 'Saturday club' of Jag diehards working after hours in order to wow crowds at the 1988 Birmingham Motor Show. And wow them it did. So much so that people wanted to buy one. Jaguar would have been mad to say no.

In the course of making the one-off into something you could buy, however, things went a bit wrong. The four-wheel-steering system didn't actually work and was swiftly binned. Likewise, the show car's active aerodynamics. The four-wheel-drive system could have been done, but it would have taken a lot of time and money so it too was junked. And the one-off's mighty V12 engine was from a racing car, unsuitable for road use and had to be replaced by a V6 from an MG Metro rally car. Yes, Jag gave it a couple of turbos but a V6 is only half as impressive as a V12.

Still, at least the smaller engine meant the massive show car could be made shorter. But no one bothered to shorten the nose, spoiling the proportions, and nor did they shrink the vast girth, making the 220 a bum puckering nightmare to drive on normal roads.

The biggest failure of the XJ220, however, was that by the time it went on sale in 1992 the economy had tanked and demand was not what it been in the heady days of '88. Worse still, those who were committed to the car and had paid a £50,000 deposit to secure one were expecting a V12, four-wheel-drive engineering powerhouse. What Jaguar was now giving them was a V6, rear-wheel-drive leviathan with lights from a Rover 200. Some customers were so disappointed they took legal action against Jag for breach of contract.

Jaguar always wanted the XJ220 to be exclusive and vowed to make just 350. In the end, only 281 came down a specially created production line before the plug was pulled.

It looked dramatic and it went like stink, but the XJ220 was still the ultimate supercar failure.

BEETLE SMEETLE

The
built during

I n the aftermath of the Second World War the British dispatched a young officer called Major Ivan Hirst to a bomb damaged factory in Eastern Germany with a brief to salvage anything worth exporting and get the place closed down. Hirst found a vast plant in a poor state of repair and examples of what it once made: A strange, bulbous car with its engine at the back. These were the remains of Hitler's doomed people's car scheme and Major Hirst, seeing value in its remnants, set about reviving both factory and car.

At this point a British commission arrived to inspect the ravaged factory, headed by British car making magnate Sir William Rootes who told Hirst that he was a 'bloody fool' if he thought cars would ever be made there again. Rootes then returned to the UK where he filed his commission's report on the car itself stating, 'The vehicle does not meet the technical requirements of a motor car. As regards performance and design it is quite unattractive to the average motor car buyer. It is too ugly and noisy – a car like this will remain popular for two or three years, if that. To build the car commercially would be a completely uneconomic enterprise.'

Despite the damning verdict of the Rootes commission, the car did enter production. It became known across the world as the Volkswagen Beetle and over a 57 year life span, 21.5 million examples were made.

At the time of writing Volkswagen itself is rated by *Forbes* magazine as the most profitable car maker in the world. The Rootes Group no longer exists.

1000th **VOLKSWAGI**

MARCH 1946 coming from Assembly

TIME GENTL
PLEASE

Concept cars are generally pretty outlandish things made to wow crowds at motorshows. The idea that you could ever buy something so nutty is absurd. Yet no one told Renault this. In early 1999 they showed off a bonkers concept with huge unbroken windows, a vast glass roof and an unusual back end with a bustle that would have shamed Queen Victoria. It was called the Avantime, a name of bastardised French to signal that it was ahead of its time. Well of course it was. It was a concept car. Except that, just six months later, they said it was going into production and would be available to buy the following year.

This, unfortunately, is where the problems started. The Avantime's striking side view and airy, well-lit interior relied on the vast side windows, uninterrupted by a central pillar. And when you get rid of a car's central pillar, the whole body tends to go floppy. Then there were the vast and heavy side doors with their complicated double hinges. These were prone to dropping out of whack, like the cupboard doors on a cheap kitchen. Both problems needed sorting and doing so took longer than Renault had reckoned with. The scheduled on sale date of 2000 sailed past and the Avantime finally crept into French showrooms in late 2001, not ahead of time at all.

The man in charge of the Avantime's design said he wanted people to be 'continually astonished' as they walked around it. In fact, onlookers were just astonished to have seen one because, though Renault said it would sell 16,000 Avantimes a year, in fact just over 8,500 were made in the car's pitifully short three year life.

In a way, this was a shame. It was an honest attempt at making something different. The Avantime also inspired a *Top Gear* item in which the presenters attempted to turn one into a track car. It was one of the most useless and pointless pieces of television ever recorded. But please don't hold that against the car.

EMEN

REN 160

HY02 EZX

HONDA

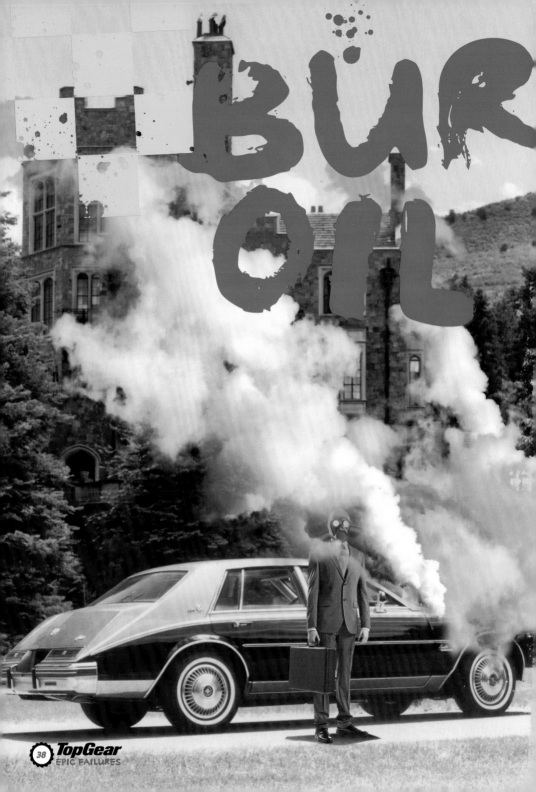

In the 1960s Americans liked big cars. Even a 90 year old maiden aunt from Idaho wasn't happy unless she was rollin' in what Europeans would consider the whole of Shropshire on wheels. But the oil crisis of the early '70s started to knock the American love of land yachts and that worried the bosses at General Motors because big cars made big profits. If everyone downsized, the same thing would happen to their bank balance. So they hit on a brilliant idea. They would make a reassuringly US-sized V8 motor, but they would have it run on diesel rather than petrol. All the size and prestige the average American customer was used to, but with the proven, dollar saving economy of diesel.

On paper, it sounded brilliant. In real life, it sounded like a barrel of oily rocks being kicked down some stairs. And noise wasn't the only problem. It was a 5.7-litre V8 that, when first fitted to various GM behemoths in 1977, made an unimpressive 125 horsepower. By 1980 that had been downgraded to a pitiful 105 horsepower and as a result, the company's flagship Cadillac Seville diesel needed 20 seconds to get to 60 and topped out at a wheezing 98mph. The average Cadillac owner could run faster. Even though the average Cadillac owner was 109 years old.

The real problem with the GM diesel V8, however, wasn't the vile noise or the woeful performance. It was simply that it didn't work. To save time and money, it was based on a similarly sized petrol V8. But diesels don't work in the same way as petrol engines and this under-specified motor spent its life smoking, belching and trying to pop off its own cylinder head.

Strangely enough, Americans didn't much fancy buying a car with a noisy, sluggish, unreliable engine and sales were poor. More than that, the entire sorry tale put America off diesel cars and to this day diesel is a hard sell in America. Which, given some of the rattly, noisy horrors Europe has had to put up with in the last 30 years, might be no bad thing.

BRÜMMIE LOGIC

In May 2000 a quartet of Midlands businessmen bought MG and Rover from BMW for a tenner and set to work on a plan to prepare the company for the future. Ideally the list would have included practicalities such as next generation engines and a new medium sized car to replace the ancient Rover 45.

What the four Midlands businessmen and the oafish, David Brent-alike they brought in to run the place actually elected to do was to buy a small Italian sports car maker called Qvale, redesign its one, unsuccessful product and then put it on sale as a brand new MG flagship.

To the MG's credit, it was nicer looking than the failed Italian sports car it was based on, even if the body was so slatted it seemed to have been attacked with

an axe. The engine wasn't bad either, being a simple American Ford V8 giving out a reasonable amount of grunt.

There were, however, many downsides. MG's bumf spoke of how the car was made in 'the very epicentre of supercar construction', which is Modena in Italy. What they neglected to add is that whilst the basic chassis was built in Modena, the fancy carbon fibre body panels were made on the Isle of Wight and that the car was completed in an industrial unit in Birmingham. This scattered approach made assembling the SV rather complicated and also rather expensive. Which is why the basic version was almost £66,000 and the faster R model a sturdy £83,000.

At the time you could have had a Porsche 911 or a Jaguar XKR for that, both of which benefited from visibly better build quality and neither of which used the headlights from a Fiat hatchback.

As a consequence, the MG SV was never in demand and fewer than 100 were built before the whole of MG Rover collapsed in 2005. They never did get around to those new engines or the new medium sized car.

By all accounts the MG SV wasn't a bad car to drive and there was some slim logic to spending the company's tiny, tiny budget on doing it. In marketing terms, it hoped to boost their other models by creating what they call 'a halo effect'. In real world terms, however, it was what they call 'sodding idiotic'.

TOGETHER In ELECTRIC DrEAMS

Is in its American homeland, General Motors oscillates between utter dullness and world-leading braveness. The former gives us the sort of grey sludge you get given as a hire car at Orlando airport. The latter leads to things like the 1966 Oldsmobile Toronado, a 17½ foot long car with a 7-litre V8 driving the front wheels, and the 1984 Pontiac Fiero, a two seat 'commuter car' with a radical, rust-resistant plastic body and the engine in the middle.

It's this adventurous spirit that also gave us the 1996 EV1, the first purpose-built all-electric car from a major car maker. It was a brave move from a large corporation, nervously dipping its toe into a different way of making cars move about.

And like many of GM's brave moments, it wasn't without flaws. Even after a (lengthy) full charge, the car's range was hopeless, especially given the vastness of American cities. The design was super aerodynamic to make the car go as far as possible but had the pop-eyed appearance of a frog trapped under a rock. And during its life it was subject to an embarrassing recall after fears it could catch fire whilst charging. Not something you wanted to happen in your garage whilst you slept.

In the end, GM spent millions promoting the EV1 but made it available in only a handful of American cities and built just 1,100 or so before production ended in 1999.

Yet none of this is why the EV1 is a top failure because, despite its problems, the EV1 was a huge hit amongst its small band of drivers. Trouble is, these smitten early adopters didn't own the cars because they were leased from, and remained the property of, GM itself. And the failure comes because, despite the obvious love for the car, despite the braveness of its design, despite the ingenuity of its engineering and the headstart it gave its maker over every other car company now scrabbling to get on the 21st century electric car bandwagon, GM quickly gave up on its electric dream. As the leases expired, the company took back each and every EV1 it had made, shipped them all to a secure facility deep in the Arizona desert, and quietly crushed them.

The original 1990 Honda NSX was a legend in its own lifetime. Its screaming VTEC V6 showed the benefits of modern technology like variable valve timing in an era when most rivals were barely out of carburettors. Its refinement and comfort showed that a high performance car didn't have to be hysterical and unusable every day. And because it was a Honda, it exposed the silly fragility of European rivals by being as faithful as a Swiss Labrador.

The NSX never sold in massive numbers but it did a lot to show the soul, passion and engineering brilliance that made Honda unique amongst its country's car makers. So when they killed it in 2005 you'd think a replacement would have been high on a list headed 'Things to do – urgent!!!!'. But in Japanese.

As it turned out, it was. In 2007 the boss of Honda announced that a new NSX was on the way and that, thrillingly, it would have a V10 engine. This was very exciting news. It was even more exciting when prototypes of the new car were spotted testing at the Nurburgring race track in Germany. Yes, they were covered in bin bags and stickers to conceal the final design but there was no

mistaking the long, low bonnet, the stubby tail and the unusual, vertically stacked exhausts that marked out a true supercar in waiting. In just a few months' time Honda engineers were going to show the world what they could do.

Except... they weren't. By the end of 2008 the Honda boss, the same bloke who just a year earlier said the NSX was 'necessary' for Honda, announced that the economy was looking a bit shaky and the new NSX wasn't coming soon. It wasn't coming at all. The entire thing had been cancelled. What a tease.

On the bright side, with the economic outlook a little brighter Honda has once again announced that it's working on a new NSX. Although they've been saying that for over three years and there's still no sign of it. So don't hold your breath.

ONE OFF the WRIST

In 1982 Mitsubishi came up with an ingenious new machine that blended the toughness of a 4x4 with the comfort of a car, performing the same trick as a Range Rover but for considerably less money. It was rugged, it was practical and it could be ordered with an extra pair of foldaway seats in the boot, long before the Land Rover Discovery or Volvo XC90 had been invented. Mitsubishi called it the Pajero.

The British importer didn't like the name and requested that it be renamed the Shogun for the UK. The Spanish importer really didn't like the name and insisted quite vehemently that any example imported to Spain was called the Montero. But that didn't stop Pajeros from other European nations entering Spain to howls of laughter. It didn't stop Spanish tourists spotting Pajeros whilst in other countries and sniggering loudly at them. It didn't stop a new generation of Spaniards being able to use the internet to look up the Pajero, now in its fourth iteration, and splutter with mirth at its very being.

The Mitsubishi Pajero is a perfectly decent car. But unfortunately for Mitsubishi, in Spanish 'pajero' means 'wanker'.

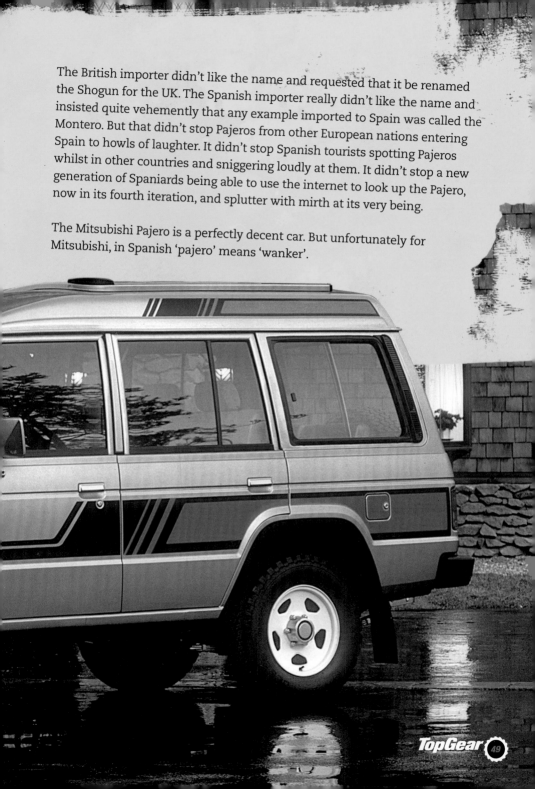

ay™ Shop by ▼
category

Search

Mastercard Lola F1 car

Click to view larger image and other views

Quantity: 1   2 available / 0 sold   **Buy it now**

Price: **£19.99**   0 watchers   **Closest offer?!**

Description   **Postage**

Item is nearly as good as new! Only used once.
~~clearly please~~ Will ship anywhere... Literally, ANYWHERE!

CARNAGE

It should be said, Lola itself was no fly-by-night. The company was founded in 1958 and had a fine history of supplying chassis' and racing know-how to some of the greatest teams and drivers in the world. They played a significant part in the development of the legendary Ford GT40, for example, and built the chassis that made Nigel Mansell American Indycar champion in his very first season. But when they decided to take a crack at F1 on their own, things didn't go well.

The team signed a $35 million deal with Mastercard in 1996 and intended to take their time getting things right before entering the 1998 F1 season. That wasn't good enough for their sponsor who wanted to see some action and insisted Lola were on the grid a year earlier. As a result, the design was done in a panic. Most F1 cars spend weeks in an aerodynamic testing facility getting details right. The number of visits Lola paid to the wind tunnel was… zero.

Against the odds, the two Mastercard Lola cars made it to Australia for the first race of the 1997 season. Granted, their in-house V10 engines weren't ready and they were using off-the-shelf Ford motors but at least they were there. Although, for many reasons, they might as well not have bothered. For example, whilst the ideal F1 car has low drag on the straights for speed and high downforce in the corners for grip the Lolas had the exact opposite. And this had a profound effect on performance. Normally in F1 the gap between the car at the front and the one at the back is measured in mere tenths of a second. In qualifying for the Aussie Grand Prix, the fastest Lola was 11 seconds slower than the man on pole. F1 employs a '107 per cent' rule based on the pole sitter's time and if you don't meet it, you can't race. The Lolas did not race that weekend.

They didn't race in Australia and they didn't race anywhere else because immediately following their F1 debut debacle Mastercard cut off funding and the whole team collapsed even before the second race of the season.

In a weird epilogue to this sorry tale, the cars still exist and in December 2013 appeared for sale on eBay. Perhaps someone bought them to point and laugh at.

STAGGERING

RRW 97H

GB

TRIUMPH

Car companies of the 1960s and '70s produced all manner of feckless, ill-conceived and ill-behaved models, many of which got the fate they deserved by rapidly rusting to nothing.

The Triumph Stag of 1970 is not one of those cars. The Stag should have been one of Britain's greatest triumphs. And indeed Triumphs. It was drop dead gorgeous. It was powered by a rumbling V8. And it had a name that just invited you to take five minutes over the A sound whilst twirling an imaginary moustache. Staaaaaaaaaaaaaaag. Even the distinctive framework that covered the cabin when the roof was down looked cool, which was a fortunate coincidence since it was really there to cover an engineering oversight that made the soft top shell all floppy without.

That wasn't the Stag's real problem, however. The real problem was Triumph's home-made and specially created engine which, with a combination of cack-handed design and shoddy build quality, fast developed a reputation for trouble. No matter how throbbing the exhaust note and how brisk the performance, neither could be enjoyed if the bloody engine had overheated again.

The Stag should have been a global smash hit. Instead, it was sunk almost immediately by a bad reputation. Triumph and its masters at British Leyland knew there were problems. They just didn't, or couldn't, spend the money to fix them. As a result the Stag sold in small numbers until it was killed off in 1977.

These days, however, Stagists have worked out how to fix the car's inherent problems. And the name still sounds tremendous if you say it properly. Staaaaaaaaaaaaaaaaaaaaaaaaaaaaaaag.

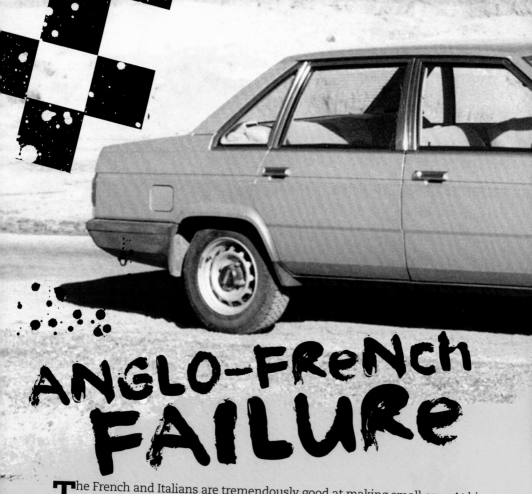

ANGLO-FRENCH FAILURE

The French and Italians are tremendously good at making small cars. At big cars, not so much. In fact, French and Italian big cars, even well designed and engineered ones, never attract any customers beyond their homeland civil service chauffeur fleets and wilfully contrary eccentrics.

Even by these low standards, however, the French-made Talbot Tagora was an epic failure. This vast, and vastly unpopular, car was conceived on the watch of American car making giant Chrysler which had created its own European division by taking over Rootes of Britain and Simca of France and then forcing them into unholy union. As a result of this uneasy Anglo-French marriage, the Tagora was engineered just outside Paris whilst its styling was confected at a Chrysler design centre in Coventry. And what styling it was, being so boxy that it seemed to have been designed on an Etch-a-Sketch. The interior was even more breathtaking, being as sparsely minimalist as a Swedish prison cell.

Unfortunately, before this brutal tribute to the power of the ruler could be finished, Chrysler sank into financial difficulties at home and flogged its entire Euro operation to the Peugeot-Citroen Group for just one dollar. The new French owners immediately made their mark on the Tagora project, imposing upon it their own V6 engine and the suspension from their 505 saloon. Neither of these things helped since the new engine required a stretched nose whilst the carry-over rear suspension was slightly too narrow for the body, both changes doing nothing for the car's appearance.

Worse yet, when the Tagora went on sale it was in direct competition with two members of its own family, the Citroen CX (which was very stylish) and the Peugeot 505 (which was designed to fit its own back axle). Since the Tagora wasn't either of these things, it was always playing third fiddle and the bosses at Peugeot treated the car like the unloved step-child it was, denying it any investment and hoping it would go away.

And in 1983, after barely three years in production, it did just that. If the Tagora is remembered, and mostly it isn't, it's not only as one of history's most angular cars but also as one of its biggest failures.

LEWIS HAMILTWRONG

1995 – 10 year old Lewis Hamilton approaches McLaren boss Ron Dennis and says that one day he wants to drive for McLaren.

1998 – Lewis Hamilton signs up for a young driver programme run by McLaren.

2007 – Lewis Hamilton makes his F1 debut driving for McLaren.

2008 – Lewis Hamilton becomes Formula 1 world champion for McLaren.

2013 – Lewis Hamilton needs new tyres during the Malaysian Grand Prix and pulls into the pit marked McLaren.
Lewis Hamilton had signed for Mercedes that season and no longer drove for McLaren.

Still, it's nice to see old mates occasionally.

GOLF PaNTS

The original 1970s Golf GTI set the template for the hot hatchback with its brisk performance, crisp handling and racy design details, all wrapped in a practical car you could use every day.

The second generation GTI added a little more space, a little more performance and, because it was now the '80s, the option of a model with a fashionable 16-valve engine, but otherwise preserved the formula of zesty fun in a sensible shell.

Then, in 1993, Volkswagen announced the third generation Golf and things went very wrong. The normal mk3 Golf was a disappointing car. It looked fat, it was badly equipped and build quality wasn't up to usual VW standards. Owners were frequently reminded of this last problem by a glovebox lid that would fall open of its own accord, giving regular passengers a bruised medical condition known as 'mark three knee'. The flagship GTI suffered from all of these problems and didn't even have performance on its side because it had a measly 115 horsepower, just three more than its much lighter predecessor. The vim and vigour of the Golf GTI had gone.

MK III Golf

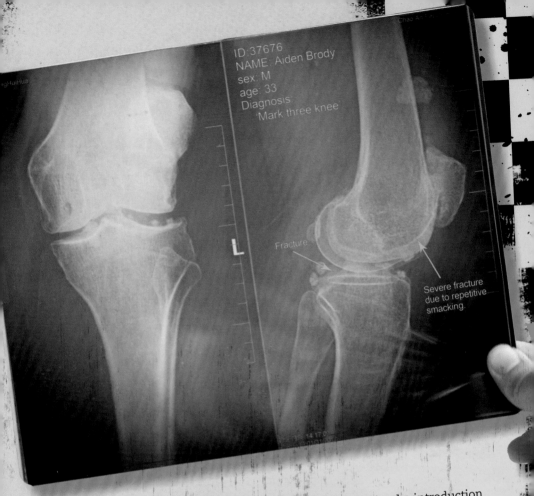

ID:37676
NAME: Aiden Brody
sex: M
age: 33
Diagnosis:
'Mark three knee'

L

Fracture

Severe fracture
due to repetitive
smacking.

And it didn't come back for the following mk4 version, despite the introduction of a gruntier 150 horsepower turbocharged engine. Yes, it was reasonably brisk but the fourth generation GTI felt lumpen, like its tyres were full of water. The non-turbo version was even worse. In fact, in most countries this 115 horsepower dullard wasn't even called a GTI. The British importer insisted on it and the cars arrived with the GTI badge wrapped in plastic in the glovebox. Some dealers didn't even bother to stick it on and then pretended going badgeless was 'good for security'. Where once Golf GTI stood for zing and excitement, this was a very undignified turn of events.

Happily, in 2004 Volkswagen announced a fifth generation GTI which brought back some of the joy and zest of the original. But for 11 long years it was definitely resting.

STOP HUMMER

In 1983 a company called AM General won a US government contract to replace the familiar Jeep with a brand-new, all-purpose military hack. It was known as the High Mobility Multipurpose Wheeled Vehicle or HMMWV and soon became known as the Humvee.

In 1992, after several years of planning and some persistent badgering from phlegm-voiced Hollywood lunk Arnold Schwarzenegger, AM General announced a civilian version of the Humvee which it called the Hummer.

The Hummer had leather seats and shiny paintwork, but was still the size of a warehouse and a little crude for anyone not engaged in actual warfare. But over in Detroit, GM could see that Hummer was a marketing opportunity waiting to happen and bought up the name. AM General continued to make the original Hummer, now renamed the H1, and GM designed two little sisters, the H2 and H3, which looked a bit like the full-fat version, but were based on existing, civilian SUVs and didn't need a parking space the size of Wales.

TIME

The cars were sold from a new chain of Hummer dealerships that looked like designer Nissen huts crouching behind a giant H. It was like being trapped inside Schwarzenegger's fantasy land. And, as it turned out, not many people wanted that. American petrol prices began to rise, an SUV backlash gathered pace and the whole Hummer endeavour looked as embarrassing as bellowing 'IT'S HAMMERTIME!' in a stranger's face.

Sales went from poor to terrible and in 2009, as GM floundered in the face of bankruptcy, the company announced that Hummer was to be shuttered. No tears were shed. Meanwhile, Humvees are still used by the US military. Because that's what they were designed for.

BACK TO THE FAILURE

What we have here is something pretty unique: A triple level failure of man, car maker and actual car.

Let's start with John Z. Delorean himself, a lunk jawed self-styled maverick who paid his dues working for GM then threw off the corporate shackles to kick back against Detroit's lazy, expendable products. Delorean wanted to create a car that would last and wouldn't change appearance every year to make the previous model look out of date. Except John Z. was always a hustler and his grand ideas were paid for with other people's money. When that ran out, he turned in desperation to a doomed cocaine deal that was really an FBI setup. Only pleas of foul play and entrapment kept him out of prison. Instead, he became a born again Christian, got baptised in his own swimming pool, and spent the rest of his life slowly selling off his various multi-million dollar properties to pay his legal bills. He died in 2005.

Then there was Delorean the company. Set up to build the dream car designed by its titular founder, it was baseless until the British government offered a substantial cash incentive to build a brand-new factory in a high unemployment area of Belfast. The firm paid Lotus £10m to develop the car itself but its other accounts were murkier than the Mariana Trench and when John Z. was busted by the Feds there was no more money to keep the place afloat. After less than two years of production, Delorean Motor Company was dead and the Belfast factory closed. Scrap merchants stripped the place and sold the heavy body stamping dies to the fishing industry so that, to this day, the equipment used to make Deloreans is weighing down nets, deep under the Atlantic. The factory itself is now owned by a French company that makes engine parts for other car makers.

Finally, there's the Delorean car. Intended to set new benchmarks for style, safety and integrity, the high minded ideals of its creator were swiftly compromised so that the finished product was little more than a bastardised Lotus Esprit powered by a wheezy Renault engine. It looked cool enough to strike up initial interest but early customers found problems like sagging gullwing doors, dicky locks that could trap you inside and a silver body that was impossible to keep clean. Demand dropped off and the underperforming Delorean died with the company of the same name.

Three years later it rode again as the star of the *Back To The Future* movie, making the Delorean famous for years to come. John Z. Delorean himself used to hang around with the Hollywood set and he would have been delighted with such product placement. Except that by the time the movie came out you couldn't buy a new Delorean and the film treated the car like the joke that it was.

PLEASE DON'T TOUCH IT.

a PAIN

Concept cars are usually wildly unrealistic pieces of pure fantasy designed to wow crowds at motor shows. They have outlandish curves and lasers for headlamps and underneath they're made of papier-mâché and Blu Tack™ and can't be driven or even taken outside if it's damp or cloudy or Thursday.

For one of these hand built, fantasyland stunners to turn, without alteration, into a real, actual car would be amazing. And that's what Audi did when it made the TT. Here was a concept car in the showroom looking exactly as it did under the bright lights of a show stand. Better in fact, because they added a little window behind the doors that stopped it resembling a smirking turtle.

It's easy to take the TT for granted now because they're everywhere, but back in 1998 it was a sleek, unique masterpiece. There was just one teeny, tiny problem.

Soon after the first owners collected their real world concept cars, reports started coming in that the TT was unintentionally more exciting than Audi had planned. In certain circumstances, notably when turning whilst slowing from high speed as coming off a motorway, the car could go into a sudden spin. The grim pictures of wrecked TTs coming in from across Europe sent its maker into a panic.

Audi asked for every TT to be temporarily returned so they could tame its tendency to pirouette with modified suspension and a tacked-on rear spoiler that sullied those unique looks. The company got a lot of kudos for creating a concept car you could buy. But they quickly realised, no one enjoys looking at a concept car if it's upside down in a field.

in the TTs

MAESTR-OH DEAR

During the mid-1970s British Leyland designed a simple, spacious and practical family hatchback which would replace the Austin Allegro and take the company roaring into the '80s. But BL didn't have any money left and it was put on hold until they attended to pressing matters like launching the Metro city car and begging the government for more cash.

When the treasury relented, the half-finished family hatchback could be completed and would go on sale in 1983 badged as the Austin Maestro. Trouble was, so much time had passed since the design was started it risked appearing stale, and Leyland bosses looked for a way to make it seem modern and exciting.

Three schemes were hatched. First of all, some engines would receive a highly advanced, computer controlled electronic carburettor. Secondly, upmarket models would be fitted with state-of-the-art polycarbonate-moulded body colour bumpers. Finally, the top of the range MG model would come with a digital dashboard and a revolutionary voice synthesizer so the car could actually speak to you if anything was wrong.

Unfortunately, when the car went on sale none of this tacked-on tech actually worked. The carburettor's digital brain sometimes went mad and decided that 'idle speed' meant a 4,000rpm frenzy. The fancy moulded bumpers cracked and shed their paint in cold weather. The voice synthesizer system – really just pre-recorded messages voiced by an actress – would issue dire warnings of things that weren't actually wrong. Although, given the lousy quality of early Maestros, she often warned of things that were too.

BL worked through many of the Maestro's problems so that the carburettors calmed down and the plastic bumpers stopped splintering. But the voice synthesizer system was a step too far. So they just threw it in the bin.

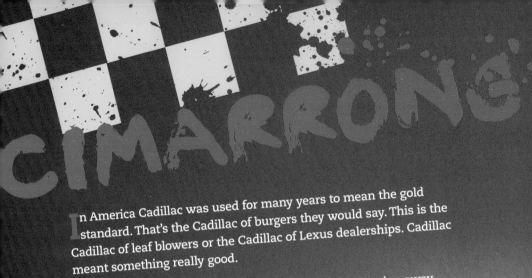

CIMARRONG

In America Cadillac was used for many years to mean the gold standard. That's the Cadillac of burgers they would say. This is the Cadillac of leaf blowers or the Cadillac of Lexus dealerships. Cadillac meant something really good.

Cadillac itself, however, spent a great deal of time frittering away its fine name with a series of ventures that undermined its standing as a mark of quality and none was worse than this, the 1981 Cadillac Cimarron.

The Cimarron was intended for people who liked the idea of a Caddy but wanted a smaller car. In itself, not a stupid notion. But the Cimarron's execution was poor, not least because it was based on the much cheaper and less prestigious box of parts also used to create the Vauxhall Cavalier.

It may have been slathered with leather, velour and deep, deep carpeting but American customers weren't as stupid as Cadillac hoped and somehow sensed that they were being asked to pay a fortune for a Euro snotbox favoured by sales reps.

Sales were way below what Cadillac hoped and by 1988 the Cimarron had been killed off without replacement. It really was the Cadillac of cheap, cynical marketing exercises.

THE PAY DRIVER'S PAY DRIVER

There are many drivers who got into Formula 1 not through supreme talent, but because they came with a big sack of cash, gratefully received by a team desperately scratching to stay afloat. These people are called pay drivers.

But Japan's Taki Inoue wasn't just a pay driver. He was the pay driver's pay driver, the one who re-wrote the rules on buying your way into a sport, wildly tipping the driving / cheque writing balance exclusively in favour of big, fat dollar signs.

Inoue's story began when he left Japan for the first time and flew to England hoping to break into motorsport. Unfortunately, someone at Heathrow misunderstood his request to find a good place for racing and put him on a coach to Newmarket racecourse.

Thanks to the backing of wealthy Japanese sponsors, Inoue eventually made it into Formula Ford, F3, Formula 3000 and finally F1 where the real comedy could begin.

Inoue's time in the big league amounted to one race in 1994 and then, incredibly, the entire 1995 season driving for the Footwork team, during which he forever cemented his reputation as the hapless Frank Spencer of motorsport.

At the '95 Monaco Grand Prix, for example, his car stalled during practice and was being towed back to the pit when it was inexplicably hit by the safety car, flipping the Footwork over and causing the unbelted Inoue to fall onto his head. During the same season, Inoue gave a press conference at which he attempted to blame his comically erratic driving on 'toothache' and suffered the humiliation of being forced to queue up for Michael Schumacher's autograph on the instructions of a wealthy benefactor, even though the two drivers were technically equals and appearing on the same grid that weekend.

Inoue's finest hour, however, came during the 1995 Hungarian Grand Prix when his poorly performing Footwork car caught fire and stopped at the side of the track. The driver jumped from his cockpit and grabbed a fire extinguisher to tackle the blaze, failing to spot the incoming fire marshal's car. Which ran him over.

Inoue survived the incident, even though organisers considered him insufficiently important to helicopter to hospital until the race was over, and he remains the only F1 driver to be run over by a saloon car during a race.

Of course, it's very easy to mock Taki Inoue for his comedy accidents, for his rubbish excuses, for his big cheques and little talent, and for his general air of failure. But, as he has proved on Twitter in recent years, there's no one in the world who likes to laugh at Taki Inoue more than Taki Inoue himself.

THE LANCIA MONTECAAA

There was much to like about the Lancia Montecarlo when it was first shown off in 1975. It was pretty, it had a fruity 2-litre twin-cam engine and it was made by one of the world's most consistently innovative and brilliant companies.

There was, however, just one tiny flaw. Because the Montecarlo was mid-engined, there wasn't a lot of weight over the front end and, for reasons known only to themselves, the designers had elected to make the servo, the brake booster fitted to all modern cars, work only on the front wheels. As a result, under anything more than moderate braking the Montecarlo's front wheels would lock in a way that could make the driver's underpants the same colour as the stylish brown leather on the seats.

Lancia realised this was a serious problem. So serious in fact that in February 1978 they stopped making the Montecarlo and went away to find a fix. In January 1980 they had found it and Montecarlo production re-started.

THEY ARE *FIXED*, RIGHT?

Journalists, engineering enthusiasts and Lancia fans couldn't wait to see what elegant and innovative solution could have taken almost two whole years to confect and pounced on the brand-new, 'series 2' Montecarlo to discover what some of Italy's top boffins had done to right the wrongs of the first generation car.

Well, what Lancia had done was take a long, hard look at the brake servo. And then they had removed it. Nothing more, nothing less. They had simply taken the thing that boosted the braking effect and thrown it away. And it took them 23 months.

Fallimento epico!

DODGE DAKOTA CONVERTIBLE

There have been convertible versions of almost every type of car. Small hatchbacks, large coupes, supercars. Even, thanks to the efforts of Clarkson, Hammond and May, a convertible people carrier and Jeremy's convertible 'sports lorry' from the Burma special. Although, strangely, both remain one-offs.

But no one had ever thought to make a convertible pick-up truck. Until 1989, that is, when Dodge of America decided to lop the top off its medium sized Dakota truck.

This was, as it turned out, an idiotic idea. Pick-ups are for hauling things around and being useful. Convertibles are for showing off and getting a tan. The two are not compatible and most Americans found the Dakota convertible as tempting as gout.

Somehow, they managed to flog almost 3,000 in its first year on sale, rapidly dropping to around 900 the year after. And how many did they sell the year after that? Eight. That's right, Dodge made just eight Dakota convertibles in 1991 and then swiftly pulled the plug on the whole sorry endeavour.

The original ads for this car proudly called it 'one of a kind'. Yeah, well there was a reason for that.

HEIL AUDI

One way to avoid an epic failure is to do a thorough background check to avoid any nasty surprises. It's something Audi's American ad agency completely forgot to do when they made a commercial to run during the 2010 Superbowl.

The ad seemed innocuous enough, depicting a near future in which acts such as using plastic bags, failing to recycle food waste and favouring non-eco bulbs are punished but in which driving an economical Audi A3 TDI gets you free pass through an environmentally orientated roadblock.

The problem was, the ad agency chose to call the uncompromising enforcers in this fictional eco future 'the green police'. Which was unfortunate, since this was also the nickname of the Ordnungspolizei or 'order police' in Nazi Germany.

Funnily enough, many Americans didn't think it appropriate to evoke Heinrich Himmler's uniformed agents of control and a significant force during the implementation of the Holocaust in order to flog a small diesel hatchback.

BURSTING the BUBBLE

In the 1950s so-called 'bubble cars' became quite popular amongst people who were sick of getting wet and cold on a motorcycle but couldn't stretch to the price and running costs of a proper car. And one of the most popular of these was the Isetta 300, a car so small and bubble-like it looked as if it might pop at any minute.

The Isetta was best known for an urban legend which said that if you drove one into your garage and stopped hard up against the back wall, you would be trapped there for the rest of time since the car's single door was on the front and the gearbox didn't have a reverse.

This isn't strictly true. Until the early '60s you could drive a bubble car on a motorcycle licence but, thanks to some arcane law, only if it had no reverse. So for people with bike licences, Isetta sold a version in which reverse was there, but blanked off. As soon as they got their car home, owners simply removed the blanking plate and never had to live in fear of starving to death in their own garage.

So that isn't the failure here. No, the real failure is that when the Mini arrived in 1959 the Isetta 300's days were numbered. Now people could have smallness and economy in something that looked and drove like a proper car. The strange little bubble was dead in the water. And this was bad news for the company that made it. Which was BMW. The British had the pesky Germans on the ropes. And Mini is still going today, stronger than ever. But owned by BMW. So the real failure here is that Britain invented something brilliant and genuinely useful and then managed to fritter it away until it was bought by the very people it almost destroyed. Dah!

PONTIAC FailBIRD

Not an uncommon reaction

There are lots of reasons why people buy cars. Because they like the colour. Because they live near the dealer. Because it's the best they can afford. But one of the biggest and simplest reasons for buying a car is because it looks nice. And here is a chilling lesson in what happens to a car when it doesn't.

The Aztek was a sort of high riding hatchback that was designed, according to the team behind it, to be deliberately polarising. We knew, they said, that from the off not everyone would like it. Unfortunately, this plan only half worked. Some people hated it. And everyone else really hated it.

The weird, beaky nose, the strange lights, the acres of inexplicable plastic cladding. It was horrible. Even the option of quirky accessories like a tailor-made tent that fitted over the back end couldn't stop the Aztek from triggering America's gag reflex.

When it came out Pontiac thought they'd sell 75,000 Azteks a year. In fact, in its first year on sale just 10,000 Americans paid their own money for one.

The Aztek made people feel queasy for five years until, in 2005, it was put out of its misery. However, in 2008 the model had a redemption when it starred as the car driven by the lead character in cult US drama series *Breaking Bad*. Although, in truth, its main job was to illustrate that the character was a bit of a loser. So the Aztek still counts as a failure.

CRASH COURSE

On lap 14 of the 2008 Singapore Grand Prix Nelson Piquet Jr lost control of his Renault F1 car as he entered turn 17 and slammed into a concrete barrier. The Brazilian driver was unhurt but the safety car was released to pause the race until the wreckage was removed from the track. At the time it seemed like an unfortunate accident but it wasn't. Piquet had crashed deliberately.

The driver subsequently alleged that the whole thing was planned by Renault F1 managing director Flavio Briatore and engineering director Pat Symonds in order to help their number one driver, Fernando Alonso, work his way up the field after qualifying in a lowly 15th place. This supposed plan dictated the exact lap, which would be just after Alonso had taken an early fuel stop, and the exact place, one of the few corners without cranes or access roads to retrieve a wrecked car, thereby forcing a safety car period that would bunch up the pack in Alonso's favour. Piquet claimed he was desperate to curry favour and have his contract renewed, which is why he played along with the ultimate example of taking one for the team. Alonso, it has always been maintained, knew nothing about it.

And, at the time, the incredible scheme worked. The crash looked like an accident and a great bit of luck for Alonso who went on to win the race. Piquet got his new contract and continued to drive for Renault. Unfortunately, part way through the following season the team grew tired of his poor performance and let him go. Piquet responded by grassing them up.

In the mess that followed Renault lost two major sponsors, Briatore and Symonds resigned and F1 was left looking rather grubby. Piquet himself wasn't punished for his part in the whole sorry affair but he hasn't worked in F1 since. And probably never will.

FUEGO. INDEED

The Renault Fuego was a very exciting car for its time. Which was, as you can tell from looking at it, the 1980s. It was sleek. It was rakish. It could be had with a power-boosting turbo. And it had, according to Jeremy Clarkson, the most comfortable seats of any car ever made in the history of everything.

Then there was its name: Fuego. Oooh, the Spanish word for fire. Yes, that really told you that this was a scorching hot coupe and no mistake.

There was just one problem. Due to a combination of iffy '80s wiring, red hot turbocharger and general French build quality, it wasn't unheard of for the Fuego to actually catch fire. Ay-ay-ay!

JAGUAR XJ-S

The Jaguar E-type is widely regarded as one of the most beautiful cars ever made. So when, in the mid-1970s, Jaguar decided to kill it off, its replacement had to be something pretty unique. And it certainly was. Just not for the reasons everyone hoped.

The new car was called the XJ-S and it looked like 19 different people had contributed ideas to the styling without ever meeting in person. The front lights were weird and oval. The back lights were strange and droopy.

The rear wheels appeared to be too far forwards. The interior was bleak and unwelcoming. And framing the back window, for no readily apparent reason, was a pair of lumpen buttresses. It was a horror.

A photographer from a major car magazine had already encountered an XJ-S prototype some two years before its announcement, but hadn't bothered to take a single shot of it because he never believed Jaguar would make something so awful. Sadly, it did.

The XJ-S was launched with great fanfare and then almost immediately sank without trace. No one wanted it. Typical '70s factory problems didn't help, such as shoddy build quality and a paint department that, for a year and a half, could only build cars in red, yellow or white. The real problem, however, was the unusual and off-putting design. Nobody wanted an XJ-S. In a desperate attempt to clear stocks, Jaguar's masters at British Leyland began offering them to middle managers as company cars. And some refused. By 1980 the situation was so desperate they stopped making the XJ-S for six whole months and nobody seemed to notice. Or care.

In fact, this story of failure has a happy ending because when the S came back it was given a nicer interior, a better engine and a wider range of colours. People started to take interest. And gradually, over its long life, it was improved and updated until it became a very nice car. Today, even early ones suddenly look rather good. Truth is, the original XJ-S was just a failure before its time.

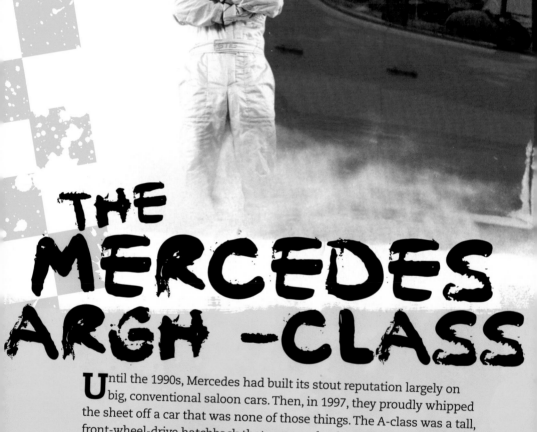

THE MERCEDES ARGH -CLASS

Until the 1990s, Mercedes had built its stout reputation largely on big, conventional saloon cars. Then, in 1997, they proudly whipped the sheet off a car that was none of those things. The A-class was a tall, front-wheel-drive hatchback that managed to be shorter than a Ford Fiesta yet more spacious than a Golf. It achieved this feat by having a false floor, under which was a cavity into which all the mechanical parts were crammed, thereby making it the first car in history to have a cellar. As a piece of design and engineering, it was ingenious.

Mercedes looked to be onto a winner until a Swedish magazine put an A-class through one of their standard procedures called the Elk Test in which the car is made to swerve violently, as if trying to avoid a big hairy thing with antlers that could make a real mess of your bodywork. It's an important concern for people in Scandinavia and most cars manage it just fine. The A-class did not manage fine. In fact, it fell over.

Merc's first response was to deny there was a problem. They rapidly followed this by admitting that, yes, okay, there might be a little bit of a problem. And then they sheepishly asked if everyone who'd bought an A-class could please give it back for a bit so that it could be retro-fitted with new suspension settings and an electronic stability control system, all at Mercedes' considerable expense.

The A-class survived the PR nightmare and went on to sell quite well. But 'elk' remains a dirty word at Mercedes headquarters.

FORD MUSTANK

The original 1964 Ford Mustang quickly became a living legend and will be forever remembered as a rumbling, square jawed, all-American hero.

The problem with creating an icon is that either you let it soldier on until it becomes an embarrassment or you roll up your sleeves and attempt to replace it with something even better.

But when, in 1973, Ford announced the Mustang II it hadn't done either of those things. Yes, the car was brand new, and yes it was usefully lighter and more compact than the model it replaced. But in all other respects, it just seemed worse. It looked dull and apologetic rather than brash and confident and, worse still, it didn't

even have performance on its side since Ford had done the unthinkable and ditched the V8 engines that formed a major part of the Mustang legend in the first place.

The reasoning behind this was the ongoing energy crisis which had made large engined cars increasingly unfashionable. But other large engined cars weren't the Mustang. The Mustang needed all the grunt and thunder it could muster. That was half the point. And without it, the point was lost.

If the original 'Stang had been a person it would have been the sort of imposing cowboy figure that saddled up and ran the bad guys out of town. The Mustang II would have been the kind of wet who claimed to be scared of horses.

PARKING

On 31 January 1994 German car maker BMW bought the Rover Group of Britain, bagging itself not only Rover but also Land Rover, MG and Mini. Across the Home Counties moustaches twitched furiously behind copies of *The Daily Telegraph* at news of the bally Hun's latest audacious move.

Even so, the Germans seemed like benign masters, handing over sacks of cash for car development and generally letting the British get on with things. But this was a mistake. Rover wasn't used to having an adequate budget, nor did it have much recent experience of designing a car on its own.

Their first major new car, the Rover 75, was announced with great fanfare but sales were disappointing. The Germans blamed the British for quality problems. The British blamed the Germans for insisting it looked as retro as the tea room at Chatsworth House.

Anglo-German relations plummeted further when BMW decided to take control of the project to re-invent the Mini. The British wanted the Germans to leave them alone. The Germans wanted the British to do as they were told and stop losing so much money.

Eventually BMW bosses panicked that the money pouring from their British operation was going to sink the whole damn company and pushed the emergency stop button.

THEY THINK IT'S all ROVER

In 1994 they'd bought Rover Group for £800m. In May 2000 they sold the Land Rover part to Ford for £1.85 billion and the Rover bit to a quartet of Brummie businessmen for a token £10. All in all, it seemed like BMW was up on the deal. But no. During their ownership they'd bankrolled the development of the Rover 75 and the new Range Rover, costing somewhere close to £2bn, they gave the tenner wielding Brummie businessmen a dowry of unsold cars, interest free loans and hard cash totalling almost another one billion, and on top of all this there were the massive costs they incurred whilst running the place for six years.

At some price, BMW washed its hands of Rover and rather wished they'd never bothered at all. Because, truth be told, they made a bit of a mess of it.

LE WRONG

Aston Martin has a history of success at the Le Mans 24 hour race. It won it outright in 1959 with the DBR1 and when it returned to racing more recently it won the GT1 class in 2007 and 2008 with a DB9-based racer. But that wasn't enough. Aston wanted to play with the big boys in the top level LMP1 class where bespoke racing prototypes duke it out for overall victory.

The car it came up with was an open roof machine called the AMR-One, powered by a purpose-built turbocharged straight-six petrol engine. Every part of this car seemed to be quite unlike what the other top teams were fielding in 2011 but no matter, Aston clearly knew what it was doing.

In a pre-Le Mans warm up race called the Six Hours of Castellet the AMR-One was alarmingly off the pace, finishing a woeful 29th and then being humiliatingly excluded from classification because it hadn't completed 70 per cent of race distance.

Aston withdrew from the following 1,000km Of Spa event and concentrated on getting a two car entry ready for the main event at Le Mans.

The big weekend arrived and British hopes were pinned to the two plucky Astons. So qualifying could have gone a bit better than 22nd and 25th but not to worry. Le Mans is a long race and there would be plenty of time in the next 24 hours to make up places.

Except, as it turns out, there wasn't. The first AMR-One completed just two laps before it retired from the race. The second car did rather better, staying on the timing screens for a full four hours, even though for most of that time it was being worked on in the pits. When the team admitted defeat and withdrew it, the car had completed a total of four laps.

And that was that. After two complete and very public failures, the AMR-One never raced again. It had been an unmitigated and embarrassing disaster. Still, say what you want about Aston's racing team but at least they know when to cut their losses.

TEE VEE ARSE

TVR had rather a good time in the '90s selling loud, unruly sports cars, mostly to loud, unruly city types who wanted to spend their weekends feeling raw power with a flex of their right boat shoe. And the glory days of the Griffith, Chimaera and Cerbera thundered on into the 2000s until one day in 2004 the boss of TVR, a perma-smoking no-nonsense chap called Peter Wheeler, abruptly sold the entire place to a strange Russian business boy.

The new owner was called Nikolai Smolenski and he was, by dint of being just 23, Russia's youngest millionaire. He was also, rumour had it, a big fan of sports cars. Well of course he was. He'd only just stopped zooming Corgi ones around the rug.

At first all seemed well. The new Sagaris sports car went on sale and conformed to the usual TVR formula of a very loud and powerful engine in a very light and slightly smelly fibreglass shell. Yet changes were afoot at TVR's Blackpool factory. Under the Peter Wheeler regime the cars gave a lot of bang for the buck and if you complained that the doors didn't fit or that your engine had gone pop, Wheeler himself might tell you to stop being such a big baby. But Smolenski had other ideas and, whilst claiming he was going to improve quality, he quietly put prices up. This didn't go down well. People who bought the cars liked that they were good value and that owning one involved an element of Russian roulette. They didn't like an actual Russian changing this. More than that, they liked that the cars were made in the image of the Marlboro chuffing bloke in charge and once he'd been replaced by some oligarch's son, it rather took the shine off. TVR sales slumped and in 2006 the company closed for good.

Meanwhile, Nikolai Smolenski disappeared from view. Perhaps he'd gone off to buy a train set.

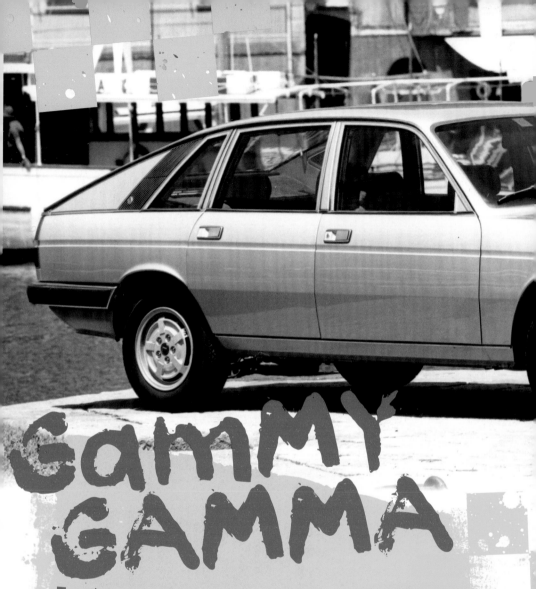

Gammy GAMMA

Lancia is a company with a long and proud engineering heritage. Unfortunately, it seemed to forget such things when it designed this, the flagship Gamma saloon of 1976.

For starters, it had the shape of a hatchback but was in fact a saloon. This disappointed anyone who wanted a large hatchback, because it wasn't, and anyone who wanted a large saloon, because it looked like it wasn't.

Then there was the engine, a brand-new design built to a flat four configuration a bit like a Porsche. Or a VW Beetle. On paper it promised smooth power and a low centre of gravity for better handling. In real life, that paper would be sodden with the oil and overheated water that piddled out of it on a regular basis.

Worse still, the power steering pump was driven off one of the fragile engine's cam belts, a brave piece of design that meant if you innocently used full lock whilst the engine was cold, the belt would pop off and the entire engine would noisily and expensively destroy itself.

Still, as well as the strange looking saloon there was a very striking Gamma coupe, which at least had the benefit of giving you something nice to look at whilst you waited for the AA.

CADDY SHACK

Some time in the 1980s Cadillac looked with envy at the Mercedes SL and decided what it too needed was a top-of-the-line two seater sports car. Accordingly, they made a call to Pininfarina, the much-respected Italian styling house, and asked them to whip up a suitable design. Not only that, they asked the Italians to build it for them. But not all of it. No, it was rather more complicated than that.

When the car, now called the Allanté, went into production in 1986 it was with the help of three specially adapted Boeing 747 freighters, which every week would fly American-made floorpans, air conditioning systems, seats and electronics from the US to Italy so that Pininfarina could mate them with the body and interior. Then the trimmed shells would be loaded onto the same 747s and flown back to Detroit to be fitted with the engine and suspension. It was an insane and expensive way to make a car.

Cadillac could have stomached such a hilariously complicated system if the Allanté had worked as a flagship and flown out of showrooms. But it didn't. Anyone not put off by the eye watering price was soon dissuaded from Allanté ownership by an early reputation for problems including major leaks around the convertible top. In fear of getting their toupees wet, target customers ran back to the Mercedes showroom.

The Allanté never sold in the numbers Cadillac had hoped and, because it was so complicated to make, is rumoured to have lost the company a fortune over its seven year life. Which is only to be expected when you create a production line that's 9,000 miles long.

MINIMISING PROFIT

The original Mini was a revelation when it came out. Here in the starchy world of 1959 was a smart, compact, economical car that tempted people off their motorcycles and out of their stupid bubble cars. Its creators had intended it to be practical and useful, but they never foresaw that it would also become something much harder to build in; it was cool. Because of this, as the '60s became more swinging, the Mini was massively in demand.

This should have been great news for BMC, the company that made it. Indeed, BMC themselves believed it was. But their rivals at Ford weren't so sure. Their own small car, the Anglia, was a wallflower next to the cutesy Mini, but at least Ford knew they were making a stout £50 for every example they sold. They also knew the Mini was a far more complicated and advanced car. So how much could BMC be making from it? To find out, Ford bought a Mini and forensically dismantled it, calculating the cost of every single part, adding on amounts for labour, shipping, dealer margins and so on. And their very carefully considered conclusion was simple: BMC wasn't turning a profit on the Mini at all. It was selling it at a loss.

The tragedy here isn't just that Britain's biggest car maker had a runaway success on its hands and still couldn't make any money off it. The real tragedy is that one of its main rivals realised this and BMC, apparently, didn't.

BUTTON

There's much to like about Jenson Button. He seems like a good bloke. He's definitely a good driver. And, since he has owned both a Nissan GT-R and a Bugatti Veyron where many drivers settle for a diesel saloon made by their main sponsor, he's clearly got fine taste in cars.

But in 2004 he was involved in a very public and embarrassing failure when, whilst driving for the BAR-Honda F1 team, it was announced that he would leave at the end of the season and re-join Williams, the outfit that had given him his first break in the sport.

This all sounded very nice. Williams were struggling and perhaps Button would be the returning hero to take them back to the top. Ummm… no. He would be the man to take them back to their solicitor's office because, despite the announcement, the British driver was still contracted to BAR-Honda for another year. Button believed there was a loophole in his contract that allowed him to leave. BAR, having paid a lot of money for a top level driver who was now threatening to bugger off, believed otherwise.

The whole thing got rather messy, F1's Contract Recognition Board became involved, and eventually it was ruled that Button must stay with BAR for another year. Which was as awkward as saying protracted and emotional goodbyes as you leave a party only to realise you've left your jacket behind.

Actually, it was worse than that because this whole farce took place before the end of the 2004 season and Button was still driving for BAR whilst steadfastly attempting to walk out on them. So the real achievement here is that for the last few races they didn't give him chocolate shock absorbers and a fuel tank full of urine.

AEROST

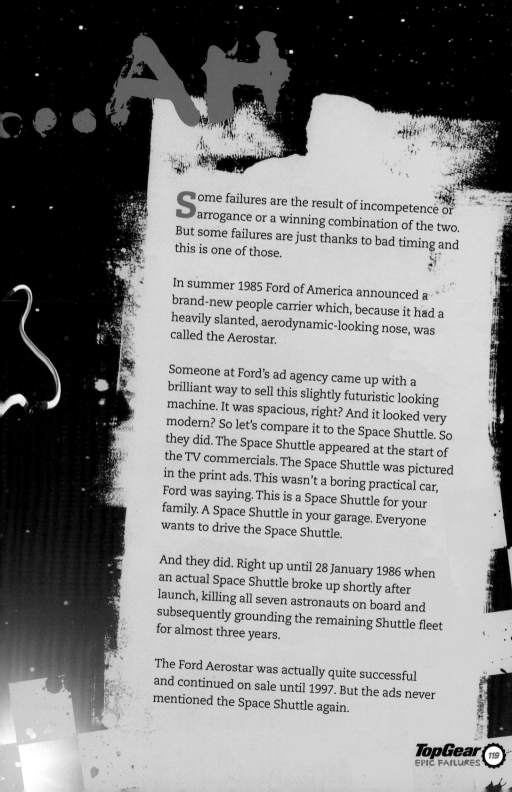

Some failures are the result of incompetence or arrogance or a winning combination of the two. But some failures are just thanks to bad timing and this is one of those.

In summer 1985 Ford of America announced a brand-new people carrier which, because it had a heavily slanted, aerodynamic-looking nose, was called the Aerostar.

Someone at Ford's ad agency came up with a brilliant way to sell this slightly futuristic looking machine. It was spacious, right? And it looked very modern? So let's compare it to the Space Shuttle. So they did. The Space Shuttle appeared at the start of the TV commercials. The Space Shuttle was pictured in the print ads. This wasn't a boring practical car, Ford was saying. This is a Space Shuttle for your family. A Space Shuttle in your garage. Everyone wants to drive the Space Shuttle.

And they did. Right up until 28 January 1986 when an actual Space Shuttle broke up shortly after launch, killing all seven astronauts on board and subsequently grounding the remaining Shuttle fleet for almost three years.

The Ford Aerostar was actually quite successful and continued on sale until 1997. But the ads never mentioned the Space Shuttle again.

TOYOTAL
RECALL

For many years, if you wanted a reliable car you bought a Toyota. This was especially true if you'd just had heart surgery because, whilst they were as dependable as a pair of Swiss scissors, Toyotas weren't the most exciting cars in the world.

All that changed in September 2009, however, when the Japanese company announced that it would be recalling a staggering 4.2 million cars in the US because of fears that the accelerator pedal could get jammed under the floor mat with unintentionally lively results.

Just a few months later, in January 2010, they issued another recall, now admitting that on certain models the throttle might stick open, floor mat or not. This time 2.3 million American Toyotas were affected, along with another 1.8 million in Europe.

For the maker of famously reliable cars, this was a disaster. Ironically, the reason Toyotas tend to be reliable is also the reason the recalls were so massive. Where other car makers might engineer new parts for each new model, Toyota found one part that worked and kept using it on dozens of models sold in vast numbers all across the world. But if that one part turned out not to work so well, that meant millions of cars needed fixing.

And fix them they did. But not before the company's justified reputation for reliability had taken a right old kicking. Still, if there was a vague risk the accelerator could jam wide open, at least you couldn't say Toyotas were boring.

THE OH-NO 80

The NSU Ro80 is one of those cars that wouldn't seem out of date today. Yet it actually comes from 1967 when it must have seemed as insanely futuristic as an astronaut's washbag.

The Ro80 had an uncommonly aerodynamic body, all round independent suspension, all round disc brakes, a 'semi-automatic' gearbox in which the clutch was operated automatically by a sensor on top of the gearlever and, most notably, a type of uniquely smooth and unusual engine called a Wankel rotary. Please stop giggling.

Unfortunately, whilst the Ro80 had an engine unlike any other car on sale, it also had problems unlike any other car on sale. Specifically, the unique engine quickly developed a reputation for guzzling fuel, burning oil and then going pop. NSU was so panicked by this bad press it began replacing engines without quibble, sometimes two, three or more in a single car.

Doing this wasn't cheap. But then developing a car this advanced hadn't been cheap either. And NSU wasn't a big car company. In fact, it was barely a car company at all, having made motorcycles and one small city car in the years leading up to this technological leap forward. Little wonder the car didn't always work as intended. And little wonder that within two years of putting the Ro80 on sale, NSU went bust.

In 1969 Audi bought up the remains. The Ro80 soldiered on to dwindling demand until 1977 when both the car and the NSU badge were killed off. Both deserved better. You're still giggling at the name of the engine aren't you?

ALL-AGGRO

The Austin Allegro isn't just the lazy comedy writer's fall-back car of choice (see also, the Reliant Robin), it's also the very definition of an epic failure.

Not because it was a bloated, pinch-faced wretch of a car that looked like a pig on wheels. Not because it came with its own set of comedy 'facts' such as claims it was more aerodynamic going backwards than forwards, which stuck to it for life, even though that particular 'fact' is true for pretty much any car with a sloping rear end. And not

because the Allegro came out in 1973 and seemed to epitomise the darkest days of the strike wracked, self-destructing British car industry that created it.

No, the real failure of the Austin Allegro is that it replaced a range of cars called the 1100 and 1300 which were small, pretty and amongst the most popular family models in Britain for many years. There was one on every street and the British loved its clever interior, its pleasant driving experience and its crisp good looks. Then the Allegro came along and threw all of that away, helping in no small way to hasten the demise of British Leyland and therefore the UK's proud industrial heritage in general.

Now that's quite a failure.

1 3 5 7 9 10 8 6 4 2

First published in 2014 by BBC Books, an imprint of Ebury Publishing
A Random House Group Company

The Random House Group Limited Reg. No. 954009

Addresses for companies within the Random House Group can be found at www.randomhouse.co.uk

A CIP catalogue record for this book is available from the British Library.

ISBN: 978 1 849 90820 7

The Random House Group Limited supports the Forest Stewardship Council® (FSC®), the leading international forestcertification organisation. Our books carrying the FSC label are printed on FSC®-certified paper. FSC is the only forest-certification scheme supported by the leading environmental organisations, including Greenpeace. Our paper procurement policy can be found at www.randomhouse.co.uk/environment

MIX
Paper from
responsible sources
FSC® C004592

Commissioning editor: Lorna Russell
Project editor: Louise McKeever
Picture researcher: Giles Chapman
Design: Amazing15
Production: Antony Heller

Colour origination by Amazing15
Printed and bound by Firmengruppe APPL, aprinta druck, Wemding, Germany.

To buy books by your favourite authors and register for offers visit www.randomhouse.co.uk

Picture credits
BBC Books would like to thank the following individuals and organizations for providing photographs and for permission to reproduce copyright material. While every effort has been made to trace and acknowledge copyright holders, we would like to apologise should there be any errors or omissions.

All images are by courtesy the manufacturers concerned and/or Giles Chapman Library, with the exception of those on pages 51 & 75, both from Sutton Photographic. Additional material © Shutterstock.